The Joy of Florida
<u>R</u> <u>V</u> Park Living

The Joy of Florida
<u>R</u> <u>V</u> Park Living

Susan K. Halverson

authorHOUSE®

AuthorHouse™
1663 Liberty Drive
Bloomington, IN 47403
www.authorhouse.com
Phone: 1-800-839-8640

Published by AuthorHouse   07/06/2012

ISBN: 978-1-4772-3669-7 (sc)
ISBN: 978-1-4772-3670-3 (e)

Library of Congress Control Number: 2012911851

Introduction

You have to understand that I was an Upper Peninsula of Michigan country girl who grew up on an 80-acre farm. There was no spring or fall, ten months of winter with over 200 inches of snow, and 30-below zero temperatures. That is why every week there was a scheduled vacation from teaching, we escaped from the cold and retreated to a warmer climate. Jamaica, Mexico, and Hawaii were our favorites, so we could enjoy sunshine, water, and sand. Cruises were another way we enjoyed warmth. As we neared my retirement, we realized the harsh Michigan winters were not for us—we wanted to play tennis, bike, and swim in balmy weather. We could not envision ourselves sitting in matching la-z-boys watching the snow fall! We loved being barefoot!

Contents

Appetizer

Cheeseball

Combine 1 jar Kraft white (pineapple) cheese, 1 jar Kraft Old English cheese, 1 jar Kraft pimento cheese, and 1 small package of Philadelphia cream cheese. Add a dash of garlic salt and a dash of onion salt. Form into a ball and roll in crushed peanuts. Cover in serving dish and refrigerate for several hours. Serve as an appetizer with your choice of crackers. Really scrumptious! Great for the driveway Happy Hour get-togethers!

Chapter I

Retirement Plans

The spring before I retired from teaching, Don and I decided to visit our friend Harold in Southwest Florida to see what paradise is all about. He would call winter evenings telling us of the beautiful 70-degree temperatures, open windows in his Air Stream, and sitting barefoot in his driveway with shorts and a T-shirt. He said life was wonderful at his RV park with all the amenities! We thought we better see for ourselves!

Since it was spring break, I had the week off from school, so we flew to Southwest Florida. We had never been to the gulf coast of Florida, only visiting the Atlantic side. We did not even know where North Fort Myers was located.

When we arrived at the RV park, it seemed so small and close-quartered. All the trailers were similar with awnings, a built-on lanai, and a paved driveway. There were a few new double wides and even some empty lots for motor homes and fifth-wheels. I could not imagine living in such small homes with our neighbors so close by.

But then our friend Harold showed us the huge pool, the tennis court, volleyball area, bocce courts, shuffleboard, and the oversided clubhouse. He elaborated on the boundless activities from the wee hours of the morning to late at night. We met his neighbors at a happy hour in the next driveway. Everyone seemed so friendly! They were all joking and enjoying the great time together. No stress anywhere in sight!

Every day we were there we met more wonderful residents all over 55 years of age. Everyone came from the Midwest, Canada, or New York. I never felt like a stranger! As I walked around the park, I saw how relaxing it was! It truly was like paradise! Every street had palm trees, each little home was immaculate, and the sun was always shining!

The last day we visited, I told my husband that I thought we would really enjoy spending next winter at this park. He agreed! So we took the next step. I walked up to the clubhouse, and there on the bulletin board was a "for rent" sign. I immediately called the landlady, made an appointment to see the rental, and found it was, indeed, fine for our purposes. It reminded me of spending a vacation at a cottage. Things were cozy but agreeable with us. We made the deposit and signed the three-month contract for the following winter. Wow! What would our family and friends think! Surely they would imagine we had gone off the deep end! Welcome to retirement at 55-plus!

Appetizer

Cocktail Meatballs

Mix one-fourth pound of ground chuck, one-fourth cup dry bread crumbs,1 egg, and one-half cup Parmesan cheese together. Form into one-inch balls and brown in skillet with one-fourth stick butter until cooked through. In separate sauce pan, melt a 10-ounce jar of grape jelly on low heat. Add a 12-ounce jar of chili sauce, 1 tablespoon Worcestershire sauce, one-half teaspoon garlic salt, one-eighth teaspoon pepper, and one-fourth cup light cream. Heat and combine with meatballs. (Yields 40 meatballs) Serve warm as an appetizer with colored toothpicks. Perfect for get-togethers! Sweet and yummy!

Chapter II

The Rental

The rest of the school year flew by with closing up my classroom, giving away everything to the students I had taught for many years, retirement parties, and the summer ahead!

When we told our family and friends we were going to Florida for January through March, they thought we were crazy! Summer blended into fall and soon it was Christmas! We had decided to leave on December 28th. The day before, we shut off the water, turned down the heat, and loaded up the car with everything from a crock pot and cookbooks, to bathing suits and shorts. We even had two one-speed Schwinn bikes on a bike rack on the back of the car, so we could not even get into the trunk until we reached Florida. That night we stayed in a motel, allowing us to get an early start! When we awoke, everything was covered with ice—the car, the bikes, and the motel parking lot! We barely got out of the driveway, which was such an icy slope!

The first day we drove to Ann Arbor, Michigan, where we spent the night with the kids celebrating Christmas!

Gifts included dominos and rummikub—which flew open in the back seat of the car before leaving. This meant all of the tiles were strewn throughout the baggage and remained that way until we reached Florida!

It took two more days to reach North Fort Myers, including cars honking and motorists pointing at our bikes that were hitting bottom on every bump, the high scary winding mountains of Kentucky and Tennessee, the ice storms with salt covering the entire car and the bikes, but warmer temperatures every day of the trip!

We finally arrived at our little rental on New Year's Eve! What a trip—1,980 miles! We had not been in the trunk of our car for four days! Our car and bikes were so grubby everything being unloaded was covered with brown dirt. We truly felt like vagrants!

While we were unloading the car, we could hear music! Sure enough, the clubhouse was bouncing with a huge New Year's Eve dance and party! What a sweet welcome! We knew we had made the right choice!

When we finally crawled into bed, we were so tired we must have passed out! In the morning I awoke to something tickling my toes! When I pulled back the sheets, I saw a tiny gecko wiggling around. I have never moved so quickly in my life, screaming and running down the hallway! My husband did not know what was happening! By the time I had nerve enough to check out the bed, the little critter was gone! We never saw him again!

Getting used to the rental took some time! Everything had to be arranged in order to fit! I was always bumping my head on cabinets or drawers, and trying to make more room! I learned quickly that you never flush the toilet when you are ready to shower, or you will be scalded for life!

I also learned that you rattle a door before you open it to scare the critters! One Sunday afternoon my husband was reading the newspaper in the lanai when I decided to shake out the rug by the back door. When I opened it, to my dismay, there was a three-foot long black snake. He looked at me and slithered right between my legs and into the lanai. I could not believe it! I screamed for Don to do something! He just looked up from his newspaper like "What can I do?" I screamed again and ran for a broom. The snake hurried to hide behind the entertainment center with me after it still howling. My back neighbor ran in to see if I were a victim of domestic violence! He summoned the neighbors' children to come to my rescue. They arrived with long rubber gloves over their forearms! When they moved the furniture away from the wall, the snake crawled behind the stairs! Now we were stuck! The concrete stairs were immobile! The boys stuffed the sides with paper, and left! I could not believe I was staying in a house with a three-foot long reptile! The glass sliding door between the lanai and the main floor was locked, but I dreamt about snakes for a week! We never found him again!

One evening I was ready to shower, and when I turned on the faucet, the entire fixture came off in my hand! The gush of water sent me reeling to the back of the tub getting me soaked. I yelled for Don! When he came in, half of the tub was already filled with water and me inside! He ran to Bob our next door neighbor to help shut off the water! Bob arrived in his red plaid pajamas! No one knew where the water shut-off was. When they entered a clothes closet, they found the washer and dryer shut-offs, but not for the bathroom. Finally after crawling under the trailer in the dark, they found the right valve! What a relief! The showers for the rest of the week were at the clubhouse until the landlady got ours repaired!

It took some getting used to but soon we knew we could only go down the hallway single file, and that the windows needed to be closed or the neighbor's air conditioner would be too loud to bear and the hot air would come right into our bedroom!

Our neighbors Bob and Theresa were so kind! They invited us to their weekly happy hour! I was so excited I prepared my favorite cheeseball in a beautiful silver serving dish! When we arrived, we found the driveway decorated with lawn chairs and little tables! About thirty people came on foot or with their three-wheel bikes. There were coolers everywhere! The couples brought their favorite beverages and appetizers, and sat right in Bob and Theresa's driveway in a circle. They all talked and laughed until it got too dark to see! What a wonderful time! Every week was a different driveway and a new host couple! Some weeks tables were set up, and it was a complete meal, including birthday parties. One time the entire street was closed for a block party, complete with chicken dinner, games, and music (a keyboard was set up in the middle of the street). No one needed a reason to have a party! Every day was a celebration!

Each day was busy with water aerobics, tennis, bocce, shuffleboard, potlucks, musical shows, and card games! The winter sped by!

Before we knew it, the end of March had arrived! What were we to do about next winter! Should we stay at the RV park!

We agreed that we loved the people and the location, so we started looking at homes to buy! Norm had a lovely home on the lake (pond), so we put money down and made an appointment at the bank for financing. That morning Don stated his jaw was sore, so he lay down for awhile. As we left for the bank, his pain returned and we had to stop right on the highway, turn around and go back home! We told Norm we needed more time! Miraculously, Don's pain disappeared!

We found another home in the park that we really liked! The couple needed to return to New York since he was ill! They made us a great offer, and we took it! Now we were Florida homeowners! Our friends and family would certainly commit us to a nursing home after hearing the news!

A Meal In Your Hand

Pasties

To make the crust combine 4 cups flour, 2 teaspoons salt, 2 teaspoons baking powder, and 1 tablespoon sugar. Add 1 3/4 cups lard. Blend until pea-size clumps form. Add one half cup cold water. Mix 1 egg and a 1 tablespoon vinegar together with a fork, and add to the crust mixture. Knead until thoroughly combined. Put into three balls and refrigerate in zip-loc bags until ready to make the pasties. (I usually double the recipe, so I make two batches of dough or six balls.)

To make the pasty filling cut up three pounds of flanksteak into cubes, 16 potatoes peeled and cubed, and 2 onions diced. Add 2 teaspoons of salt and dashes of pepper. Mix all ingredients together.

Next preheat oven to 400 degrees. You are now ready to put the pasty together. First take a wad of dough and roll out into a circle. Add one cup of mixture to one side of the dough. Fold over the dough into a half-moon shape. Crimp the non-folded edge.

Put on a baking sheet (with parchment paper). Fill the sheet with pasties and bake for 15 minutes at 400 degrees. Then bake at 350 degrees for 45 minutes. When finished baking, add a dab of margarine in a little hole on the top of the pasty. After completely cooled, wrap each pasty in aluminum foil and place in the freezer. When ready to eat, thaw in the refrigerator all day, then bake at 350 degrees for 30 minutes in the aluminum foil. They are delicious with ketchup! (The miners in Michigan used to eat them underground during lunch hour!) A double batch makes about 30 pasties. Such an easy meal when you have had a busy day at the beach!

Chapter III

Neighbors

When you live in an RV park with only 328 lots, everyone seems to be your neighbor!

Every Tuesday and Saturday morning was Coffee Hour at the clubhouse. The residents would arrive with their favorite coffee mug and a dollar. People would stand in line to select the best donut or bismark with coffee, and then sit and chat with the residents sitting next to them until announcements! Tickets were being sold for dinners or dances or shows! Trips were being promoted, and jokes abounded. The "Sunshine Lady" passed around get well cards to sign! Everyone knew everyone! Some had lived there for twenty years! It was like family!

One of my favorite neighbors was Gini. She lived in back of us in a fifth wheel! I was having trouble with our orange tree producing fruit. One morning I was out watering it when Gini happened to be in the backyard hanging up her wash on the umbrella clothesline. After exchanging "hi's", she said, "You know that tree needs some extra care." When I asked her about what I needed to do, she said, "First, you have to wake up the hormones. Just get a board and start beating it on the trunk. Then you need to sing to it." Do you know that I harvested 40 oranges from that tree after heeding her advice.

One night we had just painted our bedroom and after reassembling the bed, forgot to reinforce it! When we crawled into bed, the entire frame came crashing to the floor with a tremendous boom. The next morning there was Gini at our front door wondering what had happened the night before! Nothing gets overlooked in an RV park!

Another fun neighbor was Obi (short for O'Brien). His wife loved to get dressed up, so Obi would buy her oodles of make-up and put it on for her! One day he drove by with her in the front seat, and I thought they were going to a masquerade party! She had red circles of rouge on each cheek and the biggest red lips I have ever seen! She loved flowers, so he would buy every artificial flower possible and plant them all around their house. Just to be sure they looked nice, he would water them every day. When his wife died, he needed a passenger in his car, so he bought a huge white dog that sat in the front seat with his head hanging out the window! It looked so real, I thought he had gotten a new pet!

Another neighbor was Howard! Everything was just so with him! Every day he walked around the park three times. He was so exact that he had even counted how many steps it took to walk the perimeter. You could tell what the weather was going to be by his dress. If he had his leather jacket and gloves on with a scarf, you knew it would be around fifty degrees. If he had shorts, Argyle socks, and a straw hat on, the weather was reaching eighty degrees or warmer. He was always more accurate than the weatherman!

If you had a problem around your home, you knew who to call. Archie was the power washer, plumber, and roof painter. John was the electrician. When I had overloaded the fuse box, he told me to hammer it open, trip the switches off and on, and bang it shut again with the hammer. It worked every time! Steve was the patio maker. He would slave for days at a time on hands and knees digging in every tile. Dick was the carpenter who could put in new windows and remodel your lanai. Gordy was the sprinkling system expert. Bev was the seamstress who could whip up a new pair of curtains or your 50's poodle skirt in a jiffy. Howard and Bob were the barbers if you wanted a haircut and a story. If you needed furniture or household items, just call the wonderful people working the Flea Barn. Most things were just a quarter, so how could you go wrong!

If there was a joke played, you knew it was "Crazy George"! He had a back storage room with everything imaginable. He was the life of the party at clubhouse doings. Even JoAnn, his wife, did not recognize him in costume! She said it made her nervous not knowing what he was going to do!

Zuke was Harold's next door neighbor and also the businessman. Anything you wanted to buy or sell, Zuke had the connections. He even drew up quit-claim deeds if you wanted to sell your property. He was amazing!

Valerie was the "little angel" of the park! Whenever a resident had a need, Valerie was there with her homemade cards, soup, and encouragement! She was the "cookie lady" for board meetings, and the "original poet" for special events! She was the person who had a ticket for every upcoming event—roast beef dinners, shows, concerts, dances, you name it, you could buy it from her!

Joyce and Janet, the twin sisters, were the drivers of the Beach Buggy! Every week they would organize a van ride to a beach for the girls! Before 8 o'clock the vans would arrive at your driveway! You only needed five dollars, a lunch, and a beach chair. They even provided the noodles for swimming. After a lovely day of shelling, walking, swimming, tanning, and talking, the girls would return you to your driveway by 3 o'clock! What a super deal!

The park was so close knit, I could call anyone if I needed a ride to the airport, the hospital, or more! Everyone was your neighbor! Everyone was family!

Pizza Lasagna

To make the sauce brown 1 pound of ground chuck. Add 2 cans tomato soup, one-half tablespoon garlic salt, 1 1/2 teaspoons oregano, and 1 teaspoon pepper. Simmer for 15 minutes. In the meantime boil half a package of lasagna until tender. Oil a 9X13 inch pan. Place lasagna noodles on the bottom of the pan. Cover with the ground chuck sauce. Put one small container of fresh mushrooms on top. Sprinkle entire pan with Parmesan cheese. Add 8 ounces of cheddar cheese on top. Finish with 8 ounces of mozzarella cheese. Cover with aluminum foil. Store in refrigerator until ready to bake. Cook in 350 degree oven for 30 minutes or until cheese is melted. Serves 9. (Delicious with garlic toast and salad. Easy to make ahead and bring to the potluck dinners)

Chapter IV

Activities

When I thought of retirement, it was the life style experienced at our RV park. The schedule was like a 9-course meal seven days a week!

When we were sitting at the breakfast table, we would see masses of people already out and about walking and biking! Power washers could be heard by eight o'clock; vans would drive by picking up residents going golfing!

We would have to be at the tennis court by eight o'clock to play. There was one court and two benches to sit on while you waited your turn. Many times a dozen people would show up, so we had lots of time to chat! As you played doubles, you would change sides after one game, then sit down! I had a dance I would do with my partner if we won! We always had so much fun! One little lady was so short the ball would often bounce over her head, and she could not even reach it! One lady came to play with her bra on backwards! Another player's hand turned black from the old grip rubbing off from his racket! Crazy George would yell "You-hoo" to anyone in the pool, and they would answer back! Everyone had a chance to play and we always ended up laughing together!

Nine o'clock meant water aerobics, so I would take off my shirt and shorts and have my bathing suit underneath! The water aerobics ran Monday through Friday with up to thirty women attending. Alberta, the water instructor, was in her 80's and really good with the American Red Cross 40-minute routine. Every part of my body was bent and stretched. I was usually laughing and talking! The last section of the exercises included using two empty capped gallon plastic water jugs. We would use them to hold us up, and even pretend we were mermaids, sailors, and bicyclists. We knew everyone's name, and thoroughly enjoyed the company!

The clubhouse had weights and walk aerobics every morning. Computer club met at ten o'clock, and volleyball was three times a week in the morning.

Thursday mornings everyone came for shuffleboard. The ten courts were full of doubles partners. Powder was even dusted on to make the discs slide more easily. "Smiling Joe" was the man to beat! You never wanted to land your disc in the kitchen, or you would lose ten points! Every game you had a different partner! It was great fun!

Two brand new bocce courts were installed, so 30 teams signed up to play. Our partners were from Canada, and every Wednesday we would compete! I never knew where my balls would land! It was amazing that we won first place one year! One of the men even invented a gadget to measure the distance of the balls instead of a tape measure! Crowds usually gathered to watch! If I made a great shot, I would let out a whoop and a holler!

Friday was our beach day with the twins! As we arrived one day at "Little Hickory", our favorite beach, we saw a new sight! There was a wedding rehearsal! We all grabbed our colored noodles and made an archway from the shore to the parking lot, standing in our bathing suits, so the couple could walk through! They wanted us to come back the next day for the wedding and do the same thing!

Usually we put our beach chairs in a circle with our "Beach Babes" sign in the sand! Some of the girls would go shelling along the shore, some of us would walk for miles to our lookout point, and others would swim with their colored noodles. One time I was floating with my green noodle when I felt something by my leg! It was a huge manatee! I guess he thought the noodle was edible since it was green, and he came close by to see for himself. Many times the dolphins would be diving farther out from us! We always enjoyed the "whee waves" (yelling "whee" when a huge wave bounced us around)!

Lunches were adventures! One Friday my friend Priscilla was trying to eat a sandwich! Just then a seagull swooped down and grabbed part of it. She screamed, covered herself with her huge umbrella, and continued eating her sandwich! All we saw were her feet, the umbrella, and a flock of seagulls in a circle around her!

Everyone was herself at the beach! The passersby thought we were a book club! We just enjoyed the water, the beachgoers, and each other's company! It was lovely! At first I thought my name needed to begin with a "J" to be with the beach group because almost everyone else's name did—Janet, Joyce, JoAnn, Judy, Joanna, and Jeannie.

Some weeks the waves were so high we would have to hold each other's hands to get in and out of the water. We would lose sunglasses, hearing aids, necklaces, rings, and even cell phones. Usually we wore our beach jewelry (plastic or already corroded pieces)! One week even my noodle fell apart into three pieces while bouncing in the waves!

Evenings were really special at the park! One Sunday a month was the ice cream social! Everyone came walking to the clubhouse carrying a bowl and a spoon. Upon entering the clubhouse, you would find rows of tables filled with residents sitting and chatting. Bob would be on stage playing jazzy tunes from all eras on the piano. Two rows of men would be standing in the back clad in homemade aprons with ice cream cones on the front holding huge ice cream scoops. Tables containing all kinds of delicious homemade cakes lined the back wall! When a number was called, that table would bound for the ice cream, usually ten or more varieties with a three-scoop limit and a piece of scrumptious cake! What more could you want!

Monday evenings you paid a quarter to play euchre (a fun card game with partners). Sometimes as many as twenty tables were going at one time. I was new to the game, so they would laugh when I would let out a whoop when I made my bid. It was so much fun playing with different partners. Some even traveled out of town to play. One time I was the scorekeeper. I got so wrapped up in the game I forgot to keep score until after the third hand! Never a dull moment!

Other nights were hand and foot, pay me, bingo, bridge, and Texas hold 'em! Residents came every night to enjoy the games! Friday night was movie night. I always brought something to eat and passed it around—chocolates, mints, popcorn! Every week we enjoyed another free movie. Sometimes we were passing around tissues to blow our noses, and sometimes we were laughing so hard we almost fell out of our chairs!

Saturday nights were show nights and dinners. Musical groups would come in to perform, but also our residents were very creative! For months at a time Kay and her performers would rehearse for the computer or fun night. One never knew if Valerie would be a chicken or Crazy George would sing a song as a lady!

Special events were organized including Larry's famous roast beef dinner, Sonny's bocce chicken fundraiser, potlucks, five-dollar Thanksgiving and Christmas dinners, and state banquets (Ohio, Indiana, Michigan, Pennsylvania, New York, and Canada).

"High Tea"

"Rusty Chevrolet"

Since we were from Michigan's Upper Peninsula, the committee asked me to come up with a skit for the Michigan snowbirds' dinner. I had a "Yooper" tape of songs about the U.P., so I chose the "Rusty Chevrolet" cut. It told of the Christmas shopping trip to Shopko! I concocted a cardboard replica of a vintage rusty blue Chevrolet pick-up. It was strapped over my shoulders to look like I was driving it. Inside I had a small box of cardboard parts (muffler, radio, carburetor, and brakes). Then I dressed for the dead of winter in my red-plaid wool hat with ear laps, wool jacket, huge snowmobile boots, oversized leather mittens, and black fake teeth when I smiled!

The night of the performance I had to wait outside until I was introduced! There I stood dressed for 30 degrees below zero carrying my rusty Chevrolet over my shoulders waiting by the swimming pool! Don, a little man in his 90's, saw me and asked a lady with him if she knew where I had come from! I just smiled at him with my black teeth and he turned away!

Everyone roared when I walked in! As the song progressed, I would throw parts of the pick-up into the audience! What a night! They wanted me to take my show on the road! The Michigan banquet was never quite the same after that.

Every Sunday morning the park had their own church service complete with a pastor, organist, and a song leader. As the residents died, an annual memorial service was held. Birthday parties were quite common.

One of the Dees in the park had a birthday celebration and her whole family dressed like bumblebees!

Other fun activities included a Christmas cookie exchange and party, a ladies' high tea, where I was dressed in a homemade silk-buttoned dress and flowered hat playing the piano while the other women enjoyed a fancy lunch dressed in fancy dresses, hats and gloves!

The residents were always collecting for the needy. Baskets of food went to the deprived for Thanksgiving and Christmas. Toys were wrapped for the children. Once a year the park had a huge sale! Everything that had been donated to the flea barn during the year was set up throughout the park in displays. I usually worked the pool room where the "good junk" was. Everything from fancy dishes, gadgets, jewelry, small appliances, and clothes were on sale. Outside was the furniture, sporting goods, shoes, books, and household items.

I could not believe how early the shoppers would come. It was barely light outside and they would be waiting at the doors. Prices were so low for such "fancy junk". I was amazed how excited everyone was for a bargain.

Near the end of the day, the prices were reduced. June, my foreman, gave me a handful of plastic grocery bags with orders to sell each bag for a dollar. Whatever the customer could fit into that bag would only cost a dollar! I had to smile because my neighbor Midge bought a bag, and then asked me to help her fit the queen-size comforter that she had been eying into the bag! I squished with all my might, and we succeeded. That was when she said she wanted to take the bedskirt, also. I have never seen plastic stretch that far before! I could not believe I sold all of the one-dollar bags. One man even bought a floor lamp with the bag covering the lamp shade!

As we were closing up business for the day, we looked for our vacuum cleaner to sweep the pool room floor. It was gone! One of the customers must have purchased it!

After the sale whatever was not sold went to Miss Mary, a little red-haired lady at Suncoast, who distributed everything to the needy. Such an awesome experience. Everyone wins!

If residents were not involved in organized activities, they set up their own. Every night there were games played at the neighbors' houses, residents sitting outside talking, people walking after dark throughout the park, and always bikers. Whether you owned a two or three-wheeled bike, you were exercising. Dogs would even get a ride in the bike baskets! Packages were delivered by Dwayne behind his three-wheeler. Food was transported by bike to the clubhouse.

No wonder people lived to be in their nineties in Florida! No one had time to feel old!

Spare Ribs

Broil 3 pounds of country styles ribs sprinkled with salt and pepper ten minutes on each side. Cut up a large onion into rings and put on the bottom of a crock pot. Place spare ribs on top of the onion rings. Mix together 2 cups ketchup, 1 cup brown sugar, one-half teaspoon sage, 1/8 teaspoon pepper, one-half teaspoon onion powder, and one-half cup water. Pour on top of the ribs. Cook the ribs on low heat in the crock pot for several hours until tender. (They are so delicious and a great way to cook when you have a busy day of activities.)

Chapter V

The Manufactured Home

It was during a Sunday night ice cream social that we met a new couple, Bill and Pat. During the conversation they mentioned they were selling their home in the park because Bill was ill and they needed to be near their family in New York. We told them we wanted to buy in the park, and so they invited us over.

We both loved the two baths, huge lanai, and newer appliances. I do not think we even noticed that everything was pink and blue! After a couple of counteroffers, we bought it! Wow! They were leaving in two weeks, and we were going home to Michigan in three weeks. It was all a blur as we got busy to move everything from the rental to the new place!

The day we signed the papers we drove together to the title company. I was worried that Bill might not make it through the ordeal. As we sat at the table, there was a stack of papers six inches thick to sign. I kept giving him water to drink. Luckily, it went smoothly!

When we got home they invited me over to be briefed on our purchase. I took a pad of paper, just in case!

Bill started dictating and before I knew it I had twelve pages of instructions on what to do. He handed me a wicker basket full of liquids, cloths, and squeegees! He said I needed to wipe down the car every day because of the dew. He handed over twelve different shoe horns for Don to use at various seasons. He assigned a special glass for every occasion. One drawer just contained his medicine. Every appliance had a different maintenance procedure. They gave me a two-drawer file cabinet with all the warranties and check lists for each appliance and fixture. He even told me to store my underwear and spices in the refrigerator when we went north for the summer. I left there felling so inadequate, I did not know if we could maintain a double wide or not!

After they left for New York, we started going from room to room discarding what we did not need. The kitchen alone had twelve metal mixing bowls, so I kept three. I have never seen so many griddles, pots and pans, and dishware. I invited all of my friends to come and take what they needed. The girls left with their arms full of kitchen utensils, gadgets, and cookbooks. I could not believe how much stuff was crammed into the kitchen cupboards.

Every wall was covered with floral pictures, lighthouses, and birds. The television was covered with ivy and twinkling lights. The back bathroom had stamps from every state stuck to the walls. Even the sliding glass door to the kitchen was decorated with stick-up Easter bunnies and colored flowers. Everything was pink or blue from cooking spatulas, lacy shower curtains, bedding, towels, and hangers, to furniture, including the Samsonite card table and padded chairs. Half of the house had pink carpeting while the other half was blue! Even the wallpaper was pink and blue!

As we drove home for the summer, we talked about possibly putting our Michigan home up for sale! We could not see ourselves going back and forth every six months. We were retired, and life needed to be simpler. After driving three days to the Upper Peninsula, we agreed that we would try to sell the Michigan home.

We went to Ace Hardware, bought a "for sale" sign, and put it on the front lawn with our telephone number. The next morning I needed to get my hair cut with my beautician, who lived down the road from us and was retiring. When I arrived at the beauty shop, she said she had noticed our sign in the yard. Another lady asked if her mother and she could come and look at it. I agreed! Later that morning they walked through the house and asked if her brother could come and view it. He walked through an hour later, stood on the front steps, and said he would take it. Wow! We had not even unpacked yet from Florida. When I asked how long we could stay, he said as long as we planted Impatiens flowers in the front of the house like last year. Then we could stay all summer. We agreed. Two weeks later the papers were signed, the cash received, the flowers planted, and we were packing again.

Since our Florida home was already furnished, we just needed our personal effects. Our new buyer had been an engineer in London, and could use everything we left, even Christmas decorations, linens, and dishes. We packed up thirty boxes, the computer, the ping pong table, the stereo, and the piano. What an easy move!

All of our winter clothing and sporting equipment would have to go. Thus, Memorial Day weekend we put everything on the front lawn and waited for passersby to stop. Hoards of people came—even my 85-year-old uncle. Everything was priced a dollar! I have never seen so many excited people! They left with carloads of stuff. By the end of the day the grass was worn out. I laughed so hard watching shoppers try on neckwarmers on top of their heads for hats, A-shirts being worn as muscle shirts for the beach, and even a bow and arrow set to our neighbor who did not even hunt.

By the end of June we watched the United Van Lines truck load up our few possessions, and we drove again to Florida! We have never felt so free as we made the move with so few belongings.

The rest of the summer flew by as we made our new home in an RV park. We set up our ping pong table outside on the patio, so we could play every day. Gradually the pink and blue furnishings were replaced by greens and yellows.

All night we would enjoy watching our Detroit Tiger baseball team on the internet. The only problem was that we had our computer in the back bathroom, so we would have to set up the card table and chairs by the toilet to watch the game. As we played dominos, rummikub, and smear, we could cheer the team on. Our neighbors probably thought we were rather strange.

Cooking was a challenge. It would take me five hours to bake thirty pasties bending under the overhanging cupboards to roll out the dough.

Quarters were so narrow that only one person at a time could walk down the hall to the bedroom. The toilet paper roll was inside the cabinet of the sink since there was no room for it in the bathroom!

The closets were so small that everything had to be reironed before wearing!

Don loved Coke, so when it was on sale he would buy several cases at a time. The only storage place we had was under our bed. So if you peeked under there, all you would see is twelve cases of Coke!

The only place to store holiday ornaments was under the house. If you opened the little door you would see a half dozen plastic containers, gardening equipment, watering cans, and even a ladder, not to mention the occasional toad, gecko, and snake.

One did not even have to own a television or stereo to hear entertainment. The side neighbor always had music playing, the back neighbor enjoyed old movies, and I was always playing the piano.

I tried raising flowers in the front flower beds. One day after church I was watering my Impatiens in the front flower boxes when I saw a long reptile climbing out of the soil. I screamed so loudly my neighbor Marianne came over, grabbed a hoe, and started chopping up the salamander. He still escaped into the flowerbed minus a tail.

One morning I was watering my Hibiscus shrubs and noticed deep holes all around them. The manager said it was an armadillo. The solution: scatter mothballs all over. So I bought three bags of mothballs and did just that. The next morning to my horror there were three neat piles of mothballs and more holes. I told the manager I needed a trap. He said I could not do that because they were protected. He said to put worms in a bag in the hole, and the armadillo would get sick on them. I did not want to do that so I finally found Grub-X and sprinkled it on the lawn. The grubs were killed, and the armadillo sauntered to the next yard. Yeah!

Never a dull moment in an RV park with a quaint manufactured home, critters, and super neighbors!

Chili

Brown 2 pounds of ground chuck in a skillet with 3 tablespoons oil. Add 1 large chopped onion and 1 large chopped green pepper. Cook until tender. Add 1 can dark red kidney beans, 2 cans tomato soup, 2 tablespoons vinegar, 2 teaspoons salt, and 1 bay leaf. Sprinkle the following spices on top of the mixture: paprika, cumin, garlic powder, and pepper. Also sprinkle sugar on top. Stir together and cook in crock pot on low heat for several hours. A great meal anytime with salad, crackers, and cheese! Even though the weather may be 80 degrees, the chili still hits the spot!

Chapter VI

Church

Leaving Michigan meant giving up our Covenant church and the music program. I had been busy being the pianist and organist for the services, including playing for the choir. We took the piano with us to Florida, so I could play every day.

We had found a large Presbyterian church to attend, so I had helped with vacation Bible school, junior church, mid-week youth camp, and accompanied special musical numbers, but nothing on a regular basis for church services. Every time I played the piano in the lanai, residents walking by could hear me through the thin walls. Sometimes the neighbors would just sit on our patio and listen for awhile.

One Monday evening I received a knock at our door and there stood Dick, our neighbor from down the street. He said that their Good Shepherd United Methodist Church organist had died, and they needed someone to fill in this Sunday which was Easter. He told me he would give his choir director my resume, if I had one available. I hurriedly updated what I had and gave it to him. The next morning I received a call from Jackie, the choir director. She wanted to meet me. After a short talk, I was scheduled to play the organ for Easter Sunday services. Easter Monday I was told that they were considering me for the organist and pianist position. Two days later I was hired. What a unique position! What a miracle! I lived across the street from the church, so everyday I could ride my bike with my music bag to practice.

What a wonderful congregation! What great activities! Every week was an adventure. The choir practiced every week for services, in addition to a Christmas cantata and gospel night concert. There were strawberry festivals, Christmas bazaars, trash and treasure sales, movie nights, breakfasts, spaghetti dinners, ice cream socials, and ladies' luncheons. I can see why our Good Shepherd United Methodist Church is known as the friendliest church in Southwest Florida!

One afternoon I was scheduled to play for a memorial service, so I loaded up my music bag, hopped on to my bike, and rode to church. As I got off the seat, I realized my bike had been wet from the rainstorm the night before. My light green dress had a huge wet spot in the middle of the back! How could I meet people like that! I walked sideways into the choir room and hurriedly donned my choir robe. Saved!

A few weeks later I turned on the organ and as I played the foot pedals, I realized one of the notes continued to play even though my foot was not on it. It was stuck! I had to do something quickly. I pulled the pedal out and set it in back of the organ. As I continued to play, another pedal stuck. So I took that pedal out, and put it on top of the other one. In no time I had eight pedals in a heap! I had to be careful I did not fall off the organ bench into the empty space. Luckily, one of our members was a repairman, and fixed the problem before the next week of services.

One Saturday evening I was playing the organ, and my left contact lens fell out of my eye and landed between the organ pedals. As I played my offertory solo, I had to lean forward so my nose was almost touching the music, since that contact was to correct my nearsightedness. I was literally blind without that corrective lens. After the service a few of the members came up with flashlights and luckily we found the tiny blue lens.

After a year, the Saturday night pianist retired, so I was also playing for that service each week. That meant setting up special music for the services. I recruited a bagpiper, guitarists, tubas, saxophones, and musical ensembles. I even had a ten-year-old little girl sing, melting everyone's hearts!

Music makes the world go around, and our church is always teaming with music. I love practicing at church every day. I never know if I will be playing for the quilters, the care group, the setter-uppers and tear-downers, the staff, the bulletin crew, the power pointers, the kitchen crew, the little old lady in the office, or the maintenance man. Everyone is volunteering to make the world a better place with food, clothing, furniture, visitations, and even tutoring. Everyone has a job. Mine is spreading joy with music!

Swedish Spritz Cookies

Preheat oven to 400 degrees. Cream 1 cup butter and one-half cup sugar thoroughly. Add one-half teaspoon almond extract and 1 egg yolk. Finally add 2 cups flour and 1/4 teaspoon salt. Force dough through cooky press onto ungreased baking sheet into letter S's. Bake for 7 minutes. Let cool before attempting to remove from the cookie sheet. Makes about 5 dozen cookies. A true festive Swedish holiday cookie!

Chapter VII

Holidays

When you are retired, every day seems like a holiday! The seasons all blend together especially living in tropical Florida. It seemed so strange for me to start decorating in the fall to prepare for Halloween. Growing up in Northern Michigan, many times we trick-or-treated with winter jackets under our costumes. Here in Florida with 80-degree temperatures Halloween was more like the Fourth of July. However, celebrating Halloween in an RV park is quite a treat! My fall wreath was on the door and my lighted jack-o-lantern sat on the patio table. The little geckos loved running in and out of it. Everyone had decorations including flags, lawn markers, and lighted homes. The hall was bustling with activities. Chip and Sandy provided the smoking cauldron of apple juice, screeching skeletons hanging from the ceiling, huge cobwebs on the walls with giant spiders, dimly lit tables decorated with jack-o-lanterns, and Bob was on the organ playing creepy Halloween tunes. There were drawings and fun games at each table with gag prizes. Most of the residents came in costume, so no one knew the identity of each other. There was pumpkin pie ala mode for everyone. We all felt like we were youngsters again. Who says you have to be a tot to enjoy Halloween!

As Thanksgiving neared, the decorations changed from pumpkins to cornucopias and turkeys. Everyone collected food for the needy which was delivered prior to Thanksgiving. The clubhouse was again decked out for the occasion. Larry and his trusty crew cooked the turkey, potatoes, and dressing. Everyone also brought a vegetable, salad, or dessert. The feast was only five dollars. As people arrived, the walls were lined with tables of food. Who could have imagined a bigger spread on a cruise ship. All the dishes were homemade and scrumptious. As the packed hall stood to say a prayer of thanksgiving, it was overwhelming the sense of warmth and love in that room!

The football games came and went, and it was time for a swim in the pool. Since there was so much food remaining, everyone returned to the clubhouse for a supper of leftovers. What a wonderful day!

Christmas was the most unique holiday for me! As a youngster I remembered riding a bobsled to the back forty to cut down our evergreen with blizzard conditions. Here in Florida Don and I rode to Home Depot where they put the live fir tree in a stand for us, put it in our trunk, and all we had to do was set it up in the lanai. I still decorated it with Christmas music playing throughout the house. The best part was putting up decorations outside. Back in Michigan I would freeze my fingers while trying to chip the ice out of the eaves troughs to hang the lights. Then each night I would wade through two feet of snow just to turn them off and on. In Florida I had my shorts and sandals on while stringing lights in the 80-degree sunshine.

Christmas cookies were still made with Grandma's crank cookie press and Swedish recipe. Christmas cards were still written with the lighted spruce tree smelling up the house and the carols playing on the stereo.

Christmas caroling was quite different. Instead of riding on a tractor-pulled hay wagon from house to house, the residents gathered at the clubhouse and walked door to door singing songs with flashlights. Some even had lights on their hats. Everyone met at the hall for cookies and punch to end the evening.

Instead of mailing Christmas cards to the residents in the park, I brought them to the clubhouse and distributed them in alphabetical boxes. Then I could take my mail that was addressed to us. No postage due, and no waiting for mail. What a unique system!

As I walked through the park, I had to chuckle at the lighted palm trees, the pink flamingos with Santa hats, and the live poinsettia plants thriving outdoors.

Another special event was the holiday boat parade. We brought our chairs and sat by the canal while two hundred decorated boats passed by. A huge sailboat was decorated like an angel with a twenty-foot dress; Santa and his reindeer were on an over-sized cruiser, and there were even kayaks and paddles lit up like

Christmas trees. Music was everywhere. It was almost like a dream it was so magical!

The real meaning of Christmas, though, was still the same! I was still celebrating the season at Good Shepherd with the fully decorated sanctuary, the welcome Advent services, the beautiful choir cantata, the live Nativity scene, and the wonderful sharing of the Christmas spirit!

Easter was another holiday that was celebrated quite differently. Usually the weather was still wintry up north, so Easter bonnets were worn with boots and warmer coats. The Easter baskets were hidden in the house because of the conditions. As I prepared for the sunrise service at Good Shepherd, I had to be a well-prepared girl scout to survive! Being the pianist for the service meant sitting on the lawn at pre-dawn with a keyboard to play. Lights were set up for Pastor Tom, so I brought a neon light to attach to the music stand. Then picture the heavy dew on everything! That meant I better wear a coat to keep dry, and I needed a towel to cover the keyboard and music when I was not playing. The service was flowing nicely until the lights went out with the timer as the sun rose. No power for the microphones or the music. Then the neighborhood rooster started to crow. What an adventure! But Christ arose despite us! Hallelujah!

When my three-year-old granddaughter came over for Easter dinner, I gave her the empty Easter basket, and she searched for the eggs all over the yard! What a delightful day! Pure Son-shine!

Even the Fourth of July celebration was unique! I never missed a parade back home, so I could not start now. We drove fifteen miles to Pine Island because they had a parade. As we sat in our folding chairs, it seemed quite the same as always. Suddenly I realized that the floats were different. Every one was a boat or a golf cart. There was still music and candy strewn everywhere. The fireworks were spectacular over the river on a barge with patriotic music blaring. Freedom was alive!

Even though we were living in a different part of the world, holidays were celebrated with the same vibrant spirit!

Swedish Molasses Cookies

Preheat oven to 350 degrees. Cream together 1 cup margarine and 1 cup sugar. Add 1 egg and beat well. Add one-fourth cup molasses, 2 and one half cups flour plus 4 tablespoons flour, 1 and one half teaspoon baking soda, one-fourth teaspoon salt, one-third teaspoon cinnamon, three-fourths teaspoon cloves, and three-fourths teaspoon ginger. Form into teaspoon-size balls and place on cookie sheet. Flatten with the bottom of a glass dipped in flour. Bake for 8 minutes. Sprinkle sugar on top of each cookie when just out of the oven. Makes about 36 cookies. Delicious anytime!

Chapter VIII

Weather

It seems we went from one extreme to the other for weather conditions. Michigan provided us with thirty below zero temperatures (fifty below zero with a wind chill) and five hundred inches of snow October through May. Our summer was the month of July when we could swim in the frigid lakes, swat mosquitoes or flies, and vacation! As we neared retirement our bodies were ready for warmth year around. And that's what we found in Southwest Florida!

Every day included sunshine. Rarely were there clouds in the sky to hide the brightness. It was especially a welcome treat in the fall and winter. Being in water aerobics each morning at nine o'clock, I really appreciated even fifty degrees. Dressed in my bathing suit I would bike to the pool and jump into the 84-degree water. The air temperatures would just warm up from there to the seventies and eighties. The winds were balmy, and the yards were a burst of color-bright green lawns, rainbow colored flowers and shrubs, and lush palm trees everywhere.

I was thrilled being able to live in my shorts, sandals, and bathing suit! Life was so much easier. I remembered having to don winter jackets, boots, hats, neckwarmers, and gloves just to walk to the mailbox.

In Florida people were always outside walking, biking, enjoying sports, or just sitting on the patio. The only thing to remember was sunscreen!

Every day blended into the next one with the sun shining in the sky. Rarely was there even a raindrop.

Not until later summer did we begin getting some rainfall. Then it seemed you could set your clock by the rain. Every afternoon it would come around four o'clock. Then you might hear a rumble of thunder, see a strike of lightning, and feel raindrops for about an hour. That was the extent of the storm. Then the sun would emerge, everything would dry out, and the temperature would rise.

Our Northern friends and relatives felt sorry for us roasting in the heat and being devoured by mosquitoes. That was not the case. It was ninety degrees and sunshine, but the mosquitoes were not present. A county-wide sprayer took care of that. The temperatures up north were actually much warmer than what we had several days of the year.

Being located below the frost line, we rarely had cold temperatures. I remember only one morning when it was in the thirties. It was like living in the tropics every day.

The only difference in Florida is the possibility of hurricanes. Up north we only had lightning and thunder. Every day we would look at the weather report and plan our day. We knew if we heard a clap of thunder, we better seek shelter because the storm was imminent. One day the weatherman reported a tropical storm. The twins persuaded us to go with them to their sister's home that was not a manufactured home. We lowered our awnings, put our personal files in the car, and drove to her shelter. We enjoyed a wonderful four-course dinner, played card games all evening, watched the summer Olympics, and waited for the storm. We must have been quite a sight: eight adults sitting in the livingroom with three dogs and a cat! The rains and the winds came, but we were sleeping comfortably in the guest bedroom. Suddenly around three o'clock we heard a knock on the door. It seems Wilma, the cat, was trapped under our bed meowing with us sound asleep. She wanted to get out and we did not even hear her. When we arose, the storm had passed, we ate a delicious breakfast, and went home, thanking our precious hostess. That hurricane party was fun!

Because of the hurricane party, I had learned how to play hand and foot, a unique card game with two hands of cards. I was told to sit on one hand until the other hand had been played. I did just that, not knowing they were kidding! People live day by day and deal with what is given out! Each day is special and life is good!

I began to realize why everyone was smiling in Southwest Florida! Sunshine was abundant all around and became a part of your soul every day!

Peanut Blossom Cookies

Preheat oven to 375 degrees. Grease cookie sheets. Cream together one-half cup margarine and one-half cup peanut butter. Add one-half cup sugar and one-half cup brown sugar. Next add 1 unbeaten egg and 1 teaspoon vanilla. Thoroughly blend in l 3/4 cups flour,1 teaspoon soda, and one-half teaspoon salt. Roll teaspoon-size balls in sugar and put on cookie sheet. Bake for 8 minutes. Remove from oven, add Hershey's candy kiss on top of each cookie, and bake another 2 minutes. Scrumptious treat year around!

Chapter IX

The Big Move

After six years living at the RV park, one June morning we realized most of the residents had left for six months, and we were one of the few living in Florida year around. I asked Don if he ever considered a home with more room and a garage. He agreed that we were cramped. So we decided to go down the road looking for something else. We only made it a mile when we reached Pine Lakes. As the saleslady took us by golf cart to several homes, we found one we really liked—two bedrooms, walk-in closets, garage, everything newly remodeled, a view of a lake, a great patio and lanai, and abundant amenities! It was the same place where I accompanied the chorus for shows. Many of our church and chorus friends live at Pine Lakes. Plus the owners wanted to go back to Nova Scotia, so the price was right. Wow!

We went back to our little abode and decided to put our home up for sale. To the hardware store we trotted, bought a "for sale" sign, added our telephone number, and put it on our front lawn.

That afternoon a couple knocked on our door and said that they had just landed at the airport from Tennessee. Her father had recommended they drive through our park since they were retiring soon, and they wanted to see our home. After looking at it, they said they would call us later. The next day they made us an offer. We accepted! Now we needed to call Pine Lakes. Luckily, that home was still for sale, so we agreed on a price and bought it.

Meanwhile, we needed a quit-claim deed to finalize the sale of our RV residence. Our friend in Michigan agreed to draw up the papers and overnight mail them. The next day we received the deed, went to the courthouse and the license bureau with the prospective buyers, signed two papers, and received the cash. What a whirlwind! The new owners wanted to move in within the month, so we were again busy packing. Luckily, we could move into our new home in three weeks. Off we went to Publix for boxes. This move would be so much easier than the last one from Michigan.

We hired a man from Pine Lakes to help us transport our furniture, piano, computer, stereo, and personal items. We must have looked like the Beverly Hillbillies as we followed his loaded little red truck down the highway just a mile to our new home. Trip after trip resulted in success. Our new neighbor Jack even came over to help unload. The home seemed so spacious I felt like I was in a castle with only a few things to unpack. That was when, to my surprise, I opened the cabinets and drawers in every room. They were full of everything imaginable. Where would I put our belongings? Again, we filled our car with loads of items we did not need, and headed to Goodwill. We packed the garage so full, I told the moving man and his crew to take what they wanted. I had church members stop by and pick out items for themselves and trash and treasure. The whole driveway was full of discarded items for trash pick-up.

Every day I would clean and unpack another room. One day I did the closet. An actual walk-in closet! Do you know what a treat that was after our little double wide? For two hours I just sat on the floor of the walk-in closet and smiled and sang to myself! What a luxury!

Each new day resulted in fewer boxes. Finally, we were unpacked and home. It was so welcoming to be able to make pasties without banging my head on the cabinets. It was wonderful to have guests enjoy their own bedroom and bath without having to pull out the hide-a-bed and step over everyone. It was surreal to drive the car into the garage and stay out of the rain without getting my feet soaked in the puddle-filled driveway. It was lovely walking to and from rehearsals at the clubhouse along the lake by our house instead of driving in the dark, even though I needed a flashlight to keep track of Pine Cone and Skilly Skally, the two alligators who lurked on the edge of the lake. They usually plopped into the water when I would walk by!

One of the real perks was the tennis! In the RV park I had no chance to play with girls or in competition. At Pine Lakes there were three busy courts. Every month there was a tournament, so I thought I would enter. It was so much fun. The first tournament I only lost three games in all of the matches. I could not believe it. I was nicknamed Gazelle because I would run for every shot. I never knew who I would be paired with in the doubles' competition. The stands were full of spectators cheering me on. I won first place.

Another tournament I was paired with a girl named Barb. She asked where I had lived, and I said a little town in the Upper Peninsula of Michigan. She said she had been a counselor at a youth camp in Michigan years ago. To our surprise we realized she was a counselor at the same camp where I attended band camp. We laughed and sang the Camp Ba-ta-wa-ga-ma song right there on the tennis court during the match!

Another time I was playing a girl named Judy. She said they had lived in the same small Michigan town we did, and her husband was born two months before Don in the same small hospital. Life amazes me!

Now we are busy playing tennis four times a week. They even put me on the girls' tennis team for the fall. What fun!

I still continue my water aerobics with the empty gallon jugs. One of the girls who had lived at the RV park also moved to Pine Lakes. She wanted to continue the exercises, so I agreed to lead the aerobics for her and a few of her artist friends. Every time we are exercising two older gentlemen are doing their walking in the pool. To entertain us they sing many of the old-time favorites—"Five Foot Two" and "Show Me The Way

To Go Home", adding extra verses. By the time we are finished, we are all in stitches laughing and exercising together.

Since I accompany the Pine Lakes chorus for their Christmas and spring shows, the word is out that I am able and willing to entertain. This winter I accompanied the Lake Fairways Women's Ensemble (The Dreamers) for their Christmas and spring show "Anything Goes", which even included a live pink panther prowling through the audience. I also played for the Heron's Glen Chorus in "Broadway Bound" with live candlesticks, teapots, and steam engines. At the clubhouse a gentleman was turning ninety-five, so his girlfriend hosted a birthday party where I accompanied a six-foot-two leprechaun singing "O Johnny Boy"! If there is a wedding or a memorial service, I usually am the organist or pianist. I even was instructed to play "Satin Dolls" at a funeral. Every day is an adventure. Laughter and smiles always abound.

Another new twist to life is living in a cul-de-sac! What a terrific way to spend retirement. Our next door neighbors have thrown the most wonderful Halloween costume party with lighted musical decorations in every corner of their home and at least a hundred people attending.

Another neighbor had a Country Christmas party catered. His home had live evergreen boughs hanging from the ceilings and twelve decorated trees throughout the rooms.

My neighbor Jack has helped me trim and shop for new shrubs, powerwash pavers, and even spread twenty bags of mulch, along with taxiing us to and from the airport, collecting our mail, and providing a daily newspaper.

An older man in our cul-de-sac is truly amazing. Even though the ambulance has been to his home twice to bring him to the hospital, he just keeps getting better. This eighty-five-year-old gentleman just drove past our home this morning in a brand new Chrysler convertible. He just got his license renewed.

Another neighbor JoAnn will stop by with warm baked goods while I am working outside. One day she brought me a chocolate bourbon cupcake with cherry frosting. Yummy!

It is so wonderful to have a neighbor when you are in distress. One evening Don and I took a bike ride. Unknowingly, we forgot our keys and locked all the doors, even the one between the garage and the house. Needless to say, when we returned, we realized we were locked out. No problem. Jack, our thoughtful neighbor, came over with a cell phone, a number of a locksmith, a newspaper, and two cold glasses of water. As my husband sat in the garage on the steps reading the paper and sipping the water, I tried to reach the locksmith. He was thirty minutes away and would charge us seventy-five dollars for a service call plus parts. We were stuck at his mercy! Meanwhile, I realized I had hidden an extra key under a special rock, so I tried it. At first it did not work, but as I jiggled it, I managed to get the door unlocked. I called the repairman to cancel the call, and we were rescued. Yeah!

The cul-de-sac is just like having your family in Florida! Everyone looks after the other, tools get borrowed, recipes are exchanged, and daily conversations occur in between homes! What a special bonding occurs!

Every day we are so thankful for the move to Pine Lakes! We thoroughly enjoy our more spacious home and feel that we are in paradise!

Frozen Fruit Cocktail Dessert

Melt a bag of large marshmallows and one-half cup milk over low heat. Add 1 large can well-drained fruit cocktail and one-half pint whipped whipping cream. Crush 18 graham crackers and combine with one-half cup melted butter. Sprinkle half of the crushed crackers on the bottom of a 9X13 inch pan. Pour in the fruit mixture. Then sprinkle rest of graham cracker mixture on top. Refrigerate for several hours. Cut into squares! A light delightful dessert for potlucks or after a night of cards at your home!

Chapter X

Conclusion

Never in a million years could I have envisioned my husband and myself spending our retirement in Florida. I thought we would be freezing in the Upper Peninsula of Michigan wearing out our la-z-boys!

My parents had always taught me to dream big. Nothing is impossible! I truly believe that miracles happen each day of our lives. God is so generous. It was a miracle that we sold our Michigan home in two days. It was a miracle we found our RV park in Southwest Florida. It was a miracle we sold that home in four days and found another in Pine Lakes. And it was a miracle I was hired as the Good Shepherd United Methodist Church pianist and organist. Life is a paradise each day with sunshine and Sonshine!

Frosted Brownies

Preheat oven to 350 degrees. Grease and flour 9X13 inch pan. Combine 2 cups sugar and 1 cup margarine. Add 3 eggs and cream thoroughly. Add one-half cup cocoa, 2 cups flour, one-half teaspoon baking powder, 1 teaspoon salt, and 1 teaspoon vanilla. Bake for 30 minutes. Top with your favorite milk chocolate frosting! Awesome taste! Perfect to serve your guests when they visit!

About the Author

Susan Halverson spent all of her pre-retirement life in the Upper Peninsula of Michigan in the little town of Iron River.

After graduating from Ferris State University, Big Rapids, Michigan, with a Bachelor of Science degree in secondary education (biology and math) and graduate work at Northern Michigan University, Marquette, Michigan, she taught at Forest Park, Crystal Falls, Michigan, for many years until her retirement.

She wrote a book entitled "The Country Sampler", reflecting her memories of growing up in the country of Upper Michigan.

Since moving to North Fort Myers, Florida, she decided to author a book on her experiences in an RV park, a completely different way of life!

Susan is married to Don Halverson, a retired coach and teacher originally from Stambaugh, Michigan, has two sons-Toby and Travis, two stepdaughters-Julie and Cindy, a stepson Pat, two daughters-in-law, Kathy and Stephanie, and three grandchildren-Kirsten, Sean, and Ava.

From a little country girl to a Florida beachcomber, life is complete!